Y0-DOI-914

Tom Hanks Coloring Book

Multiple Academy Award Winner and Most Trustworthy Actor, Forrest Gump and Saving Private Ryan Star Inspired Adult Coloring Book

Dee Ross

Tom Hanks

HANKS A LOT!

TOM
HANKS

Tom
Hanks

Happy Hanksgiving

CPSIA information can be obtained
at www.ICGtesting.com
Printed in the USA
LVHW092317181218
601006LV00003B/314/P

9 781723 713088